Coral Reefs

by Libby Romero

Table of Contents

Introduction

Earth has many interesting **habitats**. Each habitat is an environment that has its own special plants and animals. One of the most beautiful habitats on Earth is found in the ocean! This habitat is called a **coral reef.**

This book is about coral reefs.

atolls

barrier reefs

coral polyps

coral reef

fringing reefs

habitats

symbiotic

tentacles

See the Glossary on page 30.

3

Where Are Coral Reefs?

Coral reefs grow only in certain areas on Earth. Coral reefs need a lot of sunlight. They need clean, clear ocean water. The water must be warm. Coral reefs also need shallow water.

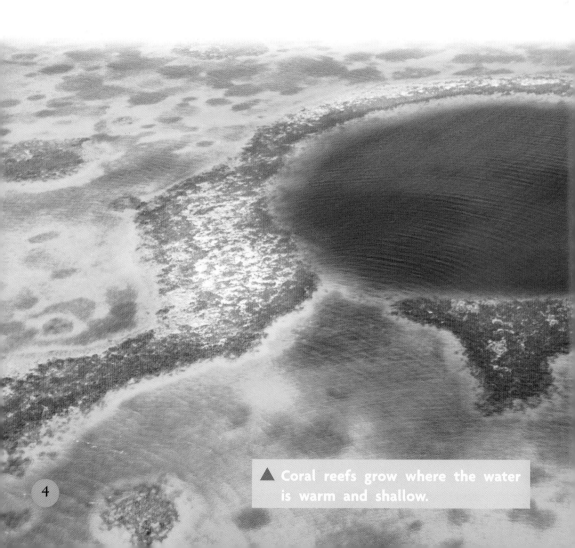

▲ Coral reefs grow where the water is warm and shallow.

Coral reefs grow in the ocean. Coral reefs grow near land.

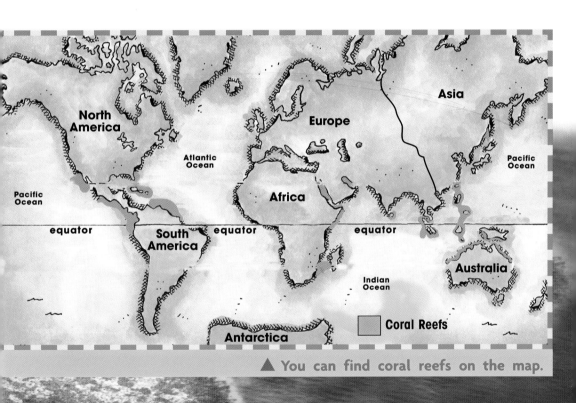

North America

Europe

Asia

Atlantic Ocean

Pacific Ocean

Pacific Ocean

Africa

equator

equator

equator

South America

Australia

Indian Ocean

Coral Reefs

Antarctica

▲ You can find coral reefs on the map.

It's a **Fact**

Coral reefs grow best during the summer when the air and water are the warmest.

There are three main types of coral reefs. **Fringing reefs** start in shallow water near land. They grow out into the ocean.

Sometimes water is between fringing reefs and land.

Land

Ocean

Reef

Ocean

Sometimes fringing reefs connect to land.

Land

Reef

Ocean

A fringing reef surrounds Green Island, Australia.

Barrier reefs are like walls between deep ocean waters and land.

The biggest coral reef in the world is the Great Barrier Reef. It is off the northeast coast of Australia.

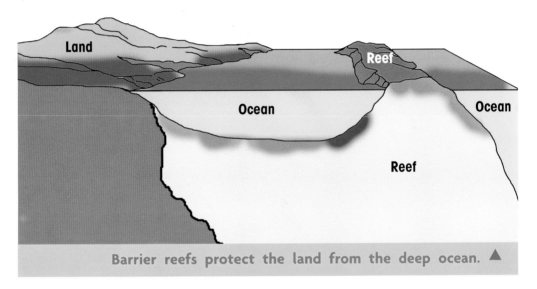

Barrier reefs protect the land from the deep ocean. ▲

This reef is part of the Great Barrier Reef. ▼

It's a Fact

Large reefs like the Great Barrier Reef are not really one large reef. They are many smaller reefs that have grown together.

Atolls are reefs that form circles. There is no land near atolls.

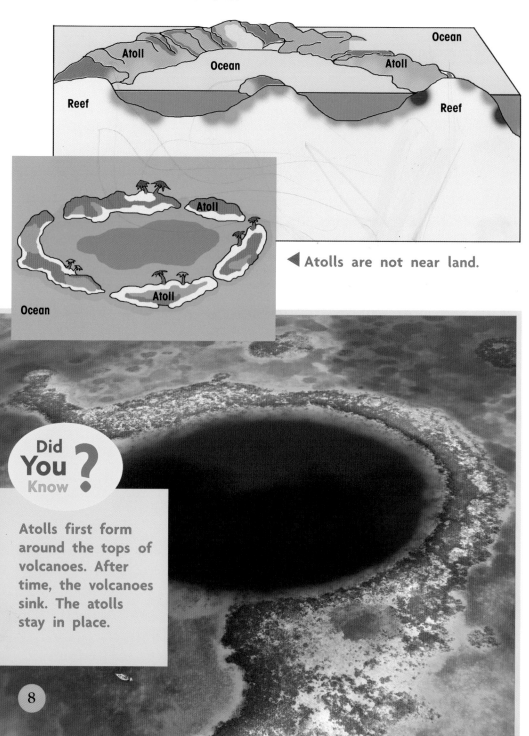

◀ Atolls are not near land.

Did You Know?

Atolls first form around the tops of volcanoes. After time, the volcanoes sink. The atolls stay in place.

How Do Coral Reefs Form?

The main builders of coral reefs are **coral polyps**. Coral polyps are tiny, tube-shaped animals. Many coral polyps are as small as pinheads. Others are as large as 10 inches (25 cm) around.

▼ Millions of coral polyps build a coral reef.

It's a Fact

Coral reefs have been on Earth for more than 240 million years.

Coral polyps have soft bodies that look like sacks. They have mouths with stinging **tentacles** around them. Coral polyps attach to the ocean floor or to other coral polyps.

Did You Know?

Coral polyps usually eat at night. Coral polyps pull their tentacles in when they are not feeding.

▲ A polyp uses its tentacles to catch food.

Coral polyps build hard skeletons around their soft bodies. These skeletons protect them. The skeletons stay in place when the coral polyps die.

New polyps grow and build skeletons on top of the old skeletons. This is how coral reefs grow.

Solve This

Many coral reefs grow about one inch (2.5 cm) a year. How many years would it take for a coral reef to grow to 4 feet (about 122 cm)?

Answer: 48 years

▲ Reefs are made of old skeletons and living coral polyps.

Each coral polyp in a coral reef goes through stages in life. This diagram shows how coral polyps grow.

The four stages of coral polyps

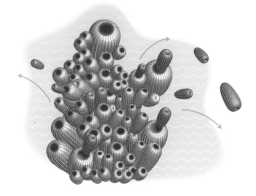

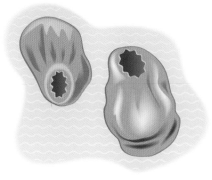

1. Adult coral produces thousands of eggs.

2. The eggs hatch. Larvae float in the water. Larvae are tiny forms of coral polyps.

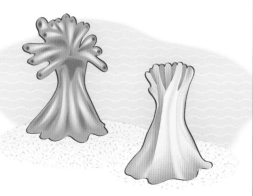

3. The larvae attach to the reef.

4. The larvae grow into adult polyps. They form skeletons to protect themselves.

What Lives in Coral Reefs?

Most coral reefs are very large. Coral reefs are full of holes and cracks. Many ocean animals and plants live in these holes and cracks.

It's a Fact

Only tropical rain forests have more different kinds of plants and animals than coral reefs.

▲ Coral reefs are great places for divers to study ocean life.

Many animals we know live on coral reefs. Shrimp, clams, and lobster live in the cracks of coral reefs. Sponges are very common in reefs. Octopuses, squid, and scallops live on or near coral reefs.

Did You Know ?

Moray eels hunt at night and eat small fish, octopuses, shrimp, and crabs.

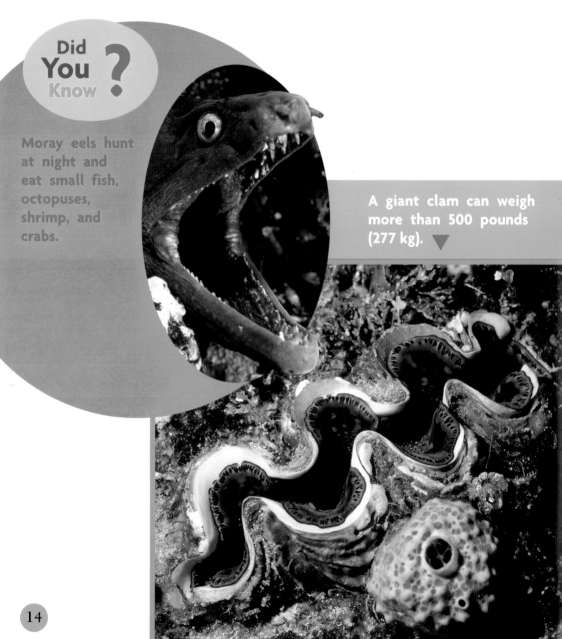

A giant clam can weigh more than 500 pounds (277 kg). ▼

Scientists are learning about other reef animals all the time. Fan worms have large heads full of tentacles. Parrotfish have strong teeth. Sea squirts take water in and squirt water out.

▲ Fan worms have tentacles that look like fans.

▲ Parrotfish use their strong teeth to eat coral.

▲ Sea squirts shoot out a stream of water when something bothers them.

Many coral reef animals need each other to survive. They have **symbiotic** relationships.

Clownfish and anemones could not live without each other. Anemones have stinging tentacles. The tentacles protect the clownfish eggs. Clownfish protect anemones from enemies.

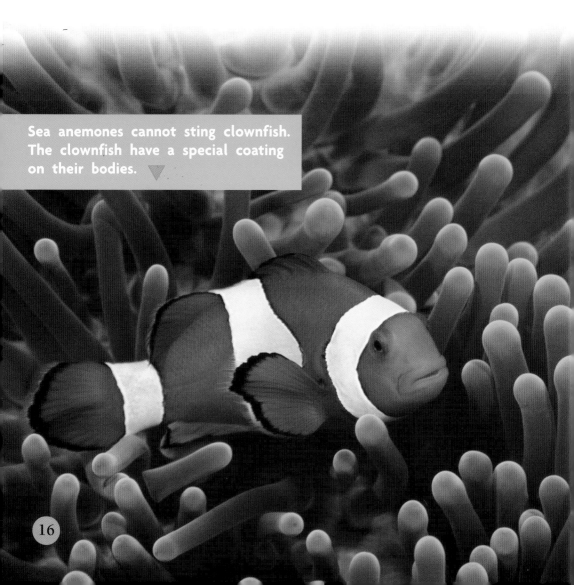

Sea anemones cannot sting clownfish. The clownfish have a special coating on their bodies. ▼

Cleaner wrasses clean the bodies of other fish. They swim inside the mouths and gills of other fish to remove waste. This waste is food for cleaner wrasses.

The other fish do not eat the cleaner wrasses. They know the cleaner wrasses are helping them.

▼ A cleaner wrasse cleans the mouth of a larger fish.

Puffer fish inflate, or make themselves larger. Then they are too big for an enemy's mouth.

Most reef fish have bright colors or stripes to blend in with the colorful reefs. Other reef fish are poisonous.

▲ A puffer fish inflates when an enemy is near.

▲ The stripes on butterfly fish make them hard to see.

▲ The spines of a colorful lionfish are poisonous.

Some reef animals find food floating in the water. They clean the water when they eat. Slingrays searchfor food on the ocean floor. Stingrays clean the sand when they eat.

▼ A stingray searches for food.

It's a Fact

The water around coral reefs is very clear and blue.

Learn More

Find out more about coral reefs. Go to this site:
The Reef Education Network
www.reef.edu.au

Why Are Coral Reefs Important to People?

Coral reefs are important to people. People eat many coral reef animals.

People from all over the world travel to coral reefs. They want to see these beautiful habitats.

▲ Some crabs, lobster, and fish come from coral reefs.

Scuba divers dive in or ▶ near coral reefs.

Coral reefs protect land along beaches. This is very important during storms. Coral reefs keep the sand on the beaches from washing away.

▲ Coral reefs protect beaches and buildings from big waves and storms.

Coral reefs also help sick people. Many important medicines come from coral reefs.

It's
a
Fact

Scientists are studying sponges for new anti-cancer medicines.

Scientists use sea whips in medicines that ease pain.

Coral reefs are easily harmed. Nature causes some of the damage.

▲ Strong waves in a hurricane can break apart large coral reefs.

Human beings cause the most damage to coral reefs. People throw trash into the oceans. This harms the reefs.

Oil spills, chemicals, and garbage kill coral. These things cover reefs. They block the sunlight that coral polyps need. Trash can also kill reef animals.

▲ Pollution has already destroyed 10% of the world's coral reefs.

Earth's population is growing all the time. Problems for coral reefs are growing, too. People are catching more fish, and reef populations are dying.

It's a Fact

More than half of the world's population lives near oceans. In the United States, more than half of the people live near oceans.

26

▲ **Building too close to oceans can hurt coral reefs.**

People visit reefs on vacations. They take coral home because it is pretty. They do not know that breaking off the coral hurts the reefs.

Coral reefs are important to us. We need to protect them.

Did You Know?

People must change how they treat coral reefs or the reefs might die.

Summary

Coral reefs are important to the animals that live there. Coral reefs are important to people.

Coral

Where Are Coral Reefs?

- shallow water
- warm, clean ocean water
- near the land
- in the ocean

Chapter 1

How Do Coral Reefs Form?

- coral polyps
- skeletons

Chapter 2

Reefs

What Lives in Coral Reefs?

ocean plants

ocean animals

Chapter 3

Why Are Coral Reefs Important to People?

food

beautiful habitats

beach protection

medicine

Chapter 4

Glossary

atolls coral reefs that
form circles

*Some **atolls** are in the
middle of the ocean.*

barrier reefs reefs between
deep ocean water and land

*The Great **Barrier Reef** is off
the coast of Australia.*

coral polyps small sea animals
that form skeletons; the skeletons
are part of coral reefs

***Coral polyps** live together and
form a coral reef.*

coral reef a special
underwater habitat for plants
and animals

*A **coral reef** is an
ocean habitat.*

fringing reefs coral reefs
that start near land

*Fringing reefs are close
to land.*

habitats places where
animals or plants naturally live
and grow

*A coral reef is a **habitat** for
a puffer fish.*

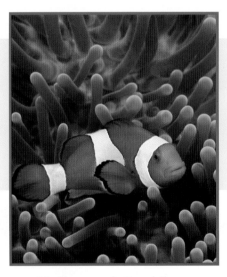

symbiotic a relationship
between two animals that
is good for at least one of
the animals

*The clownfish and the sea
anemone have a **symbiotic**
relationship.*

tentacles long, thin body parts
on some animals that are used
to grab or move

*A coral polyp uses its stinging
tentacles to catch food.*

Index